TIME-LIFE
Early Learning Program

The Family Tree

TIME
LIFE *for*
Children®

ALEXANDRIA, VIRGINIA

Note to Parents

Most young children have only a fuzzy grasp of history. *The Family Tree*, which tells the stories of the seventh birthdays of a boy, his father, and his grandfather, traces lifestyle changes of three generations in a single family. Children are introduced to the past by seeing how daily life has evolved over the last 60 years.

In each of the three birthday segments, the reader sees a cutaway of the family's house (pages 20, 42, and 48) and a panorama of their home town (pages 12, 38, and 54). Ask your child to compare the house from one generation to the next; what is different, and what is the same? Then look at the pictures of the town and ask your child the same questions.

This book is not intended as a history of all families. Rather, it offers an opportunity for you to discuss your own distinctive family history with your child. Tell your child how your family has changed over time. Look at family photos together, pointing out old-fashioned clothing, hair styles, buildings, or cars. Finally, talk about family traditions that have survived the years, making your family unique.

The Family Tree

Hi! My name is Johnny, and today is my birthday! I'm seven years old, thank you very much for asking. As soon as school is out I'm going straight home for a family celebration. We're big on birthdays in my family.

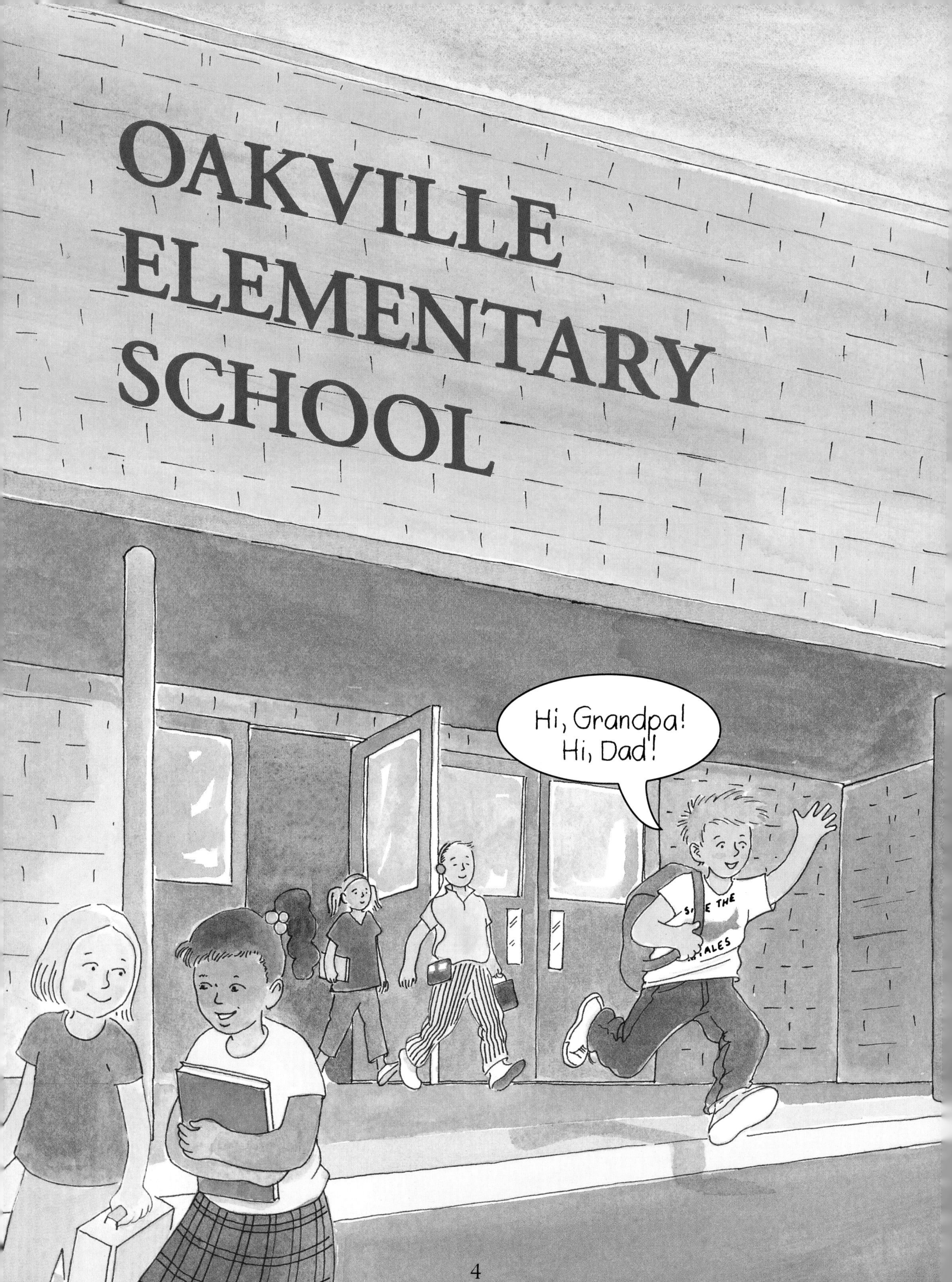
OAKVILLE ELEMENTARY SCHOOL
Hi, Grandpa! Hi, Dad!

While we wait in the car, Grandpa starts in on one of his favorite topics–the good old days when he was a boy.

Grandpa's Seventh Birthday

I woke up early and pulled on my knickers–all boys wore short pants in those days. Suddenly a heavenly smell drifted into my room. Leapin' Lizards! Fresh rhubarb muffins!

Mother baked those muffins for every birthday breakfast. That year she had a new gas stove, which we thought was very modern and spiffy. Before that, Mother had cooked all our food on a coal-burning stove.

Hurry up, Birthday Boy! Your favorite treat is ready, and your friend Mr. Peterson, the iceman, is here.

Happy birthday, Ralph!

8

We didn't have a refrigerator. Instead, we put the ice in a wooden icebox to keep our food cold. The icebox didn't run on electricity—it ran just on ice! When the ice melted, we had to buy a new block from the iceman.

I grabbed another muffin and ran outside to meet the iceman—it was my job to tell him what size ice block we needed. As usual, my little sister, Vicky, tagged along to give a carrot to Mr. Peterson's horse, Silver.

If I'd known it was your birthday, Ralph, I would have made you something—out of ice, of course!

Hurry up, Ralph. Even birthday boys have to do their chores!

My birthday happened to fall on wash day. So while I sat on the back steps eating another muffin, Mother filled the washtub, soaped the clothes with a bar of soap, and scrubbed them against a bumpy washboard.

You think that's funny? Just listen to how she dried them! She cranked the wet clothes through two roller bars called a wringer, which squeezed out the water. Then she hung them up to dry.

10

A lot of folks in town grew vegetables in their backyards. Watering our garden was another one of my jobs. But as I started to sprinkle...

Hey, Ralphie! Do you have time for a birthday spin?

My Uncle Kip had landed his biplane in the field beside our house!

Grab your schoolbooks and your lunch bag, and let's go!

Oakville was a lot smaller in those days. As soon as the plane took off, we could see the whole town laid out below us.

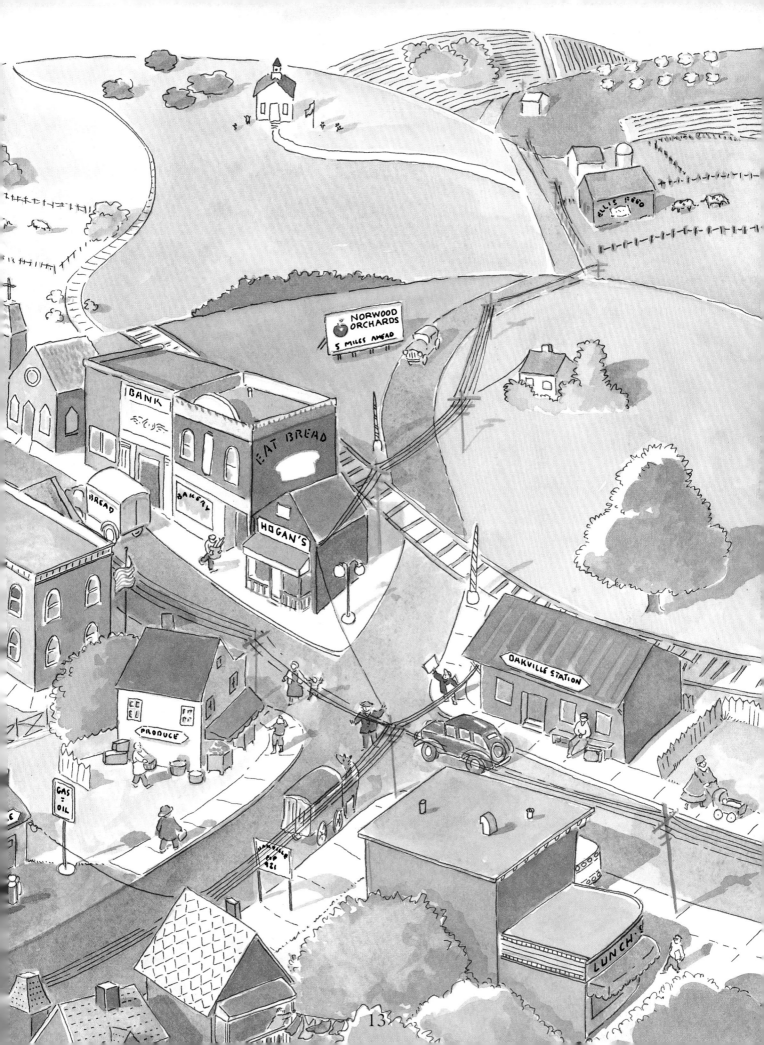

Uncle Kip landed on the field next to my school, and I skipped in right on time. No one had ever come to school in an airplane before!

Miss Kilkenny rapped her desk with a ruler to get our attention. We all stood, put our hands over our hearts, and recited the "Pledge of Allegiance."

Then, instead of sitting down, my classmates sang "Happy Birthday!" Boy, was my face red!

Our first lesson of the day was always penmanship. Miss Kilkenny wrote some letters on the blackboard, and we copied them in our books, over and over again, exactly as she had drawn them. Well...almost exactly!

We didn't use pens like you have now. We used fountain pens, which had to be refilled with ink from a bottle. It was easy to make a mess!

Black Cat INK

After school, my pals Wally, Toby, and I stopped off at the store to buy some penny candy with a birthday dime that Uncle Kip had given me. Back then, we didn't have a shopping center or a mall–we had Hogan's General Store. You could buy just about anything at Hogan's.

"May I have two red licorice whips and a sheet of candy dots, please?" I asked Mr. Hogan.

Mr. Hogan handed me the candy and then reached back into the case. "I'll throw in a birthday jawbreaker, too, Ralph!" he said.

Chewing our candy on the walk home, we watched the Red Lightning Freight Train thunder by, puffing clouds of steam. The engineer saw us waving and blew his whistle–just for us!

We didn't have to be home for a little while, so we stopped to shoot marbles in the empty lot next to the train station. It was my lucky day! I won back my favorite marble–a blue "aggie," a striped shooter that I used to hit the other marbles. I'd lost it to Toby the week before.

Then some older boys came by to play baseball.
I didn't have a glove, but they let me play anyway!
How did I do? Well, I wasn't exactly Babe Ruth, the
greatest ballplayer who ever lived, but I did get a hit.
I was one happy seven-year-old!

After the game, I ran all the way home–to my
house, that is, not home plate!

At home, my family had hidden my birthday presents all over the house. It took me a long time to find all four of them.

Mother and Father gave me a
brand-new baseball glove and ball.

My grandfather gave me a set
of baseball cards, including one
of the Sultan of Swat himself–
Babe Ruth!

My best friend, Wally, gave me a
little leather bag to hold my marbles.
He had made it himself!

And Vicky gave me a small
box that rattled when I shook it.
Inside was an acorn she had
found in the woods.

22

"It will grow into a great big oak tree," I said. And, with Vicky's help, I planted it behind the house.

23

After dinner, we all walked down to the Rialto Theater to see a picture. It was *Tarzan*, and we thought it was swell. I think everyone in Oakville heard me practicing Tarzan yells on the way home.

After the movie, we stayed up late listening to exciting stories on the radio. There were all kinds of great radio shows–*Tom Mix*, the cowboy who always shot straight, *Little Orphan Annie*, and *Jack Armstrong, the All-American Boy*–but my favorite was *Buck Rogers in the 25th Century*. I was a Buck Rogers "Solar Scout" with an official Solar Scout's Badge.

Mother finally shooed us off to bed, but I wasn't quite ready for sleep. I turned out the light, opened my curtains, and took out my Buck Rogers "Lite Blaster" flashlight. Then I flashed a goodnight message in code to Wally, whose window I could see across the street. We didn't really know any codes, but we had fun pretending.

...And that's how it was on my seventh birthday.

28

Dad's Seventh Birthday

Mom—that's your Grandma Anne, Johnny—used to wake me up at the crack of dawn so I could do my paper route. I'd jump on my bike and ride around the neighborhood delivering newspapers. It was great practice for my pitching arm!

Afterward, I rode home to–can you guess? Birthday rhubarb muffins! Mom put a candle in one, and she and Dad and my big brother, Scott, sang "Happy Birthday" to me at breakfast. Then we had to race to catch the school bus!

31

At school, we were learning all about space travel. Astronaut John Glenn had just become the first American to orbit the Earth in a space capsule. Mr. Bealer, our teacher, said that astronauts would be walking on the moon by the time our class was in high school! Since it was my birthday, he let me take home the model rocket we had made.

In the school cafeteria at lunchtime, I traded baseball cards with my friends. Roger Maris had just broken Babe Ruth's home-run record, and Jackie Robinson, the first black ballplayer in the major leagues, had been elected to the Baseball Hall of Fame. It was a big year for baseball!

Finally, the clock struck three, and I raced home to open my presents.

My grandmother gave me a pair of roller skates—the kind with metal wheels that you strap onto your shoes.

Mom gave me a real cowboy outfit with a lasso and spurs.

Scott gave me a new Chubby Checker record—"The Twist"—and said I could play it on his hi-fi!

My Aunt Vicky, Dad's sister, gave me a hula hoop.

Then Dad led me out into the backyard to see the most exciting present of all: He had built me a tree house in the oak tree that he had planted on his seventh birthday 30 years before!

Since it was my birthday, Mom let us watch a little afternoon TV. We had a black and white television set, with four channels to choose from. The picture was pretty fuzzy, so we fiddled with the antenna all the time, trying to get it just right. Scott let me pick the channel that afternoon, and he held the antenna in just the right spot.

But he didn't have to hold the antenna for long! We heard a "Beep! Beep!" out front, and there was Great-uncle Kip, revving the engine and blowing the horn of his brand-new convertible.

We roared into Oakville's new drive-in
hamburger stand. We didn't call it fast food
in those days, but it was pretty fast, all right.
We stayed in the car, and our food was
delivered to us by a waitress on roller skates!

"Say," Uncle Kip suggested, "let's talk your
parents into taking us to the drive-in movie tonight!"

So we raced back to the house to get ready for the drive-in.
Dad found blankets, Mom packed popcorn, and Scott and I
got into our pajamas—that's right, our pajamas!

The drive-in was like a huge parking lot with a giant screen at one end. We parked next to a short post, facing the screen. Dad lifted a metal box off the post and hooked it onto the car window. This was the speaker box! All the sounds and voices and music from the movie came into our car through that box! It was exciting and cozy, but...

SNACK SHACK

...when the movie got too mushy, Scott and I would go over to the swing set and play in our pajamas. Those were the days, Johnny!

As soon as we got home, Scott and I dragged our official Boy Scout sleeping bags out to the new tree house. We brought Scott's telescope to look at the stars, and we spotted one moving across the sky slowly and steadily, without twinkling–a satellite!

My Seventh Birthday

Back home, I think of all the things that have changed since Dad and Grandpa were my age.

Look back at the family house on Grandpa's seventh birthday (page 20) and Dad's seventh birthday (page 42). What has changed? What is the same?

But then I hear my family singing "Happy Birthday" in the backyard! The picnic table under Grandpa's oak tree is piled high with a big cake with candles, ice cream, and—you guessed it—fresh rhubarb muffins baked by Grandpa and Dad!

There's also a heap of presents:

A new computer geography game that lets you design cities and towns...

...a robot that turns into a rocket ship that turns into a submarine...

...a tropical rainforest endangered-species board game that makes real animal sounds...

...and a small box from Grandpa and Great-aunt Vicky!

52

53

Look back at the pictures of Oakville on pages 12 and 38.
How has the town changed since Grandpa's seventh birthday?
What has changed since Dad was seven?